Hurrah's Nest

Hurrah's Nest

Arisa White

VIRTUAL ARTISTS COLLECTIVE
http://vacpoetry.org
ISBN: 978-0-9440480-1-6

Cover art by Debby Sou Vai Keng, ink on rice paper, from the series "Days and Nights," used by permission:
http://vacpoetry.org/debbysouvaikeng

Poems in this collection have appeared in the following publications:

"Disposition for shininess," "Raw meat makes my hands aware of the skin's unravel," "To you, named the messenger of god," and "On that day," *Disposition for Shininess*. Factory Hollow Press, 2008; "Jumped," and "P.S. 21's assembly for the blackface documentary," *I Saw My Ex At a Party*. KSW Press, 2008; "The emperor's socks," *Boxcar Poetry Review*; "The small places I go," *The Altruist*; "Ribbons and Straw," *jubilat*; "The spell is broken" *Torch: Poetry, Prose and Short Stories by African American Women*; "Starved," Snowvigate.com; "It was easier to manage," *The Minnesota Review*; "Yoga," Shampoo; "Last bath" and "An albatross to us both," *Poets for Living Water*; "In the grip of dirt," *Lily: A Monthly Online Literary Review*.

To Jamar, Ibert, Kayana, Shaquana, Nigel, and Uriah.

Contents

To you, named the Messenger of God

I came into an extended family of boys who skinned knees
and rough played. Jamar, first-born in the weather of her womb.
Ibert mourned the light that drained him from her cupola.
Kayana came normal then the tonic-clonic brewed her brain.
Shaquana broke waters with six-pointed hands.
Nigel arrived on the golden bell's 12th toll, and you, Uriah

rode a love inexhaustible, inducible as Jah or art.
We're her seven wonders and sins. In nights of hell,
she gave us iced lullabies to cool our sleep.
Still I burned in the crook of her cradling, troubled
by the face we share. Her voice *sha-sha* notes
of incomplete comfort. I body myself like a kayak

and to what shore I pedal, I'm Kayana seized in epilepsy,
shaken to stillness, wake to find home is her. A blue wryness
colors this epiphany of hands, aching for the soil of her laughter.
No shaman with leaves or cowries reading godly scripts could jam
such truth into my eyes. Faraway we move in the strictness of her lines.
Ibert in Nicaragua is pulled by her moon. In the mandolin's quiet, Nigel

finds her climbing his clefts; "every good boy does fine" niggles
his ears. Strung by deft fingers, her affects linger stronger than cayenne.
She's obeah woman's curse cast when he a toddler, swells Ibert's
neck until speech is the faded note pulled from the bottle. *You liar,*
I write in Mother's Day cards for her missteps and neglect. Jamar
picks no bones; I direct the skeletons with my pens; Shaquana

with bold fonts points and shames.
Far too many times we were Nigel, unsafe in boyfriend's hands,
wilting while his skin rose in welts. No Jamar, no police
just the fusillade of 'kay, 'kay—the missing o's kept
for salvaged selves we floated away. Uriah,
you do not know the wrecks, our possible flights: Ibert,

from monkey bars, landed with broken sky in his hands. I bent
into a fetal memory, sucked the genie from my thumb. Shaquana
sprinted, her arms swinging machetes. For seconds she lifted. You are an
addition to this breath; listening to each shell in the way Nigel
studies sound, predicting how to fill holes tricking Kayana into falls,
and for what spot soft enough we lift the other's sadness. We jambeau

against collisions come low. Uriah, you are protected in Ibert's prayers;
in Jamar's, Shaquana's eyes your beauty's given back. You brown
in Nigel's sun-soaked scales, and we choral psalms from Kayana's water-vowels.

We Not Crazy, We Feeling Irie

She rolls my locks like a spliff. Her dreadlocks thick
as cattails weep to her shoulders.

It's the 80s. When my mother and I walk the streets,
strangers avoid us as if we carry a shitting stench.

Leaning into her chest, the scent of her skin
sweetens my air like a frankincense burn.

She tells me to say my ABCs, massages my head
until my scalp absorbs lavender oil.

Our hair's mat and nap is treason against granny's
straightened bob and auntie's permed curls.

They say, *No little girl should have her hair like that;
what would people think?*

My mother sings as if her tongue were raised
alongside the sea's echo.

Her Jamaican accent acquired from Rasta associations,
brings tide to steel of city living.

With the complaint that vegetarianism is starvation,
my aunt threatens to call child welfare.

What social worker would mistake grating coconuts for *ital*,
squatting on the kitchen floor, as an act of neglect?

The record player wakes Beres Hammond's vinyl silence;
his voice a warm rain when the skin asks for cooling.

She has played the same song all week. She lifts me from her lap
and gestures to dance. I spin my skirt into a parasol.

She stands, moves with waves beneath her,
an island body lit by uncovered bulbs.

I join her muted march, our locks in pendulum sway.
We two trees in the coming of winter, putting up resistance.

FOLLOW

He sits on the edge of the tub,
      her hands afraid to leave touch.

His wound a pit filled with juice
      of boiled sorrel leaves
            she covers with sterile cotton.

In his laughter the elegy
      to his back, to the hole
            she can place her left breast into.

The gunfire left behind ellipsis,
      a muted open mouth.
            He washes his hands with soap,

Rests his nerves on susurrations
      to Jah and King Selassie.

Her hands free his dreadlocks from the cap
      she crocheted red, gold, and green,
            harvests bad thoughts with coconut oil.

He says, *Da po'leece comin fi me.*
      She watches the bandage, says,
            Get rid of the gun. I'll take care of the weed.

IT WAS EASIER TO MANAGE

I started kindergarten that fall you went off to Guyana.
Granny cut off my dreadlocks. She knew how to press

and curl, ponytail, and cornrow but palm roll
locks till the roots stiffened with beeswax,

glistens like licorice, she didn't know.
For that matter, no one in the Projects knew

what to do with hair left natural, left
unparted and wild—they were afraid to touch

that unmothered part of themselves. Each snip
made each one alive and each one dead.

And if you said goodbye, it was an honest whisper,
short and fine in your throat.

She cut my hair like a boy's
who hadn't been to the barber for a month,

and I sat at the cafeteria table alone for weeks.
They couldn't make sense of me, my classmates

with their gender-proper hairstyles. I didn't
want anything to do with franks & beans,

those pucks of grilled meat. I waited at lunchtime
for peanut butter and jelly and was hesitant to eat

bread that wasn't our color. It was hard
not hearing your voice each morning,

throughout the day. And unwilling to correct them
when they said my name wrong, I gave into

the Sizzlean; the fried chicken crunched
between my teeth, I could've bitten both of your hands

for leaving me here, each finger for the gunshots that rang
the night, the footsteps running on the roof, the gravel mashed

deeper and deeper into my sleep. Flocks of butterflies
broke my skin and I was shatter where I stood,

a whole constellation of wondering if I could throw
myself to the sky, coat it with urgent wishes

you'd see that I missed you, that the barter was unfair,
that you mistook me for sheep.

WIDOWS

She was telling me I would be alone.
We shared the same "V" above our foreheads.
Granny put her bangs down,
left me at the vanity with my forthcoming mourning.

One first grade afternoon, I took the scissors,
black handles faded like her nail polish
when two weeks passed between manicures.
The widow's peak fell on her eaux de toilette.

It was remedy against a husband,
their complications with diabetes,
adulterous tongues, and crap-shoot wrists.

I was her little girlfriend, she confessed
to her Korean employers at the dry cleaners.
I sat on a box, charmed from the hoots
and husky shush of machines,
granny putting starched creases in trousers.

She slept on one side, on one pillow. The habit held
a partition in place, she let me temporarily break.
I spooned her body while the 11 o'clock news aired.
Asleep before the weather report, she carried me
to my own bed. Every night she wanted me to learn this.

LAST BATH
for Jamar

The bubbles die and there is a different life ahead of us.

The once-continent turns to islands; fish school close to our bellies.

Seeing under water is a collision on my eyes.

The water takes out my braids, turns cold because I didn't want them like seaweed.

You turn the shower on and there's no point worrying.

We drown in a storm of beads. Impatient beads

that don't hold still for threading, and sharks come at the wrong time.

I'm past pruning but still must save my tail.

It's our monkey-bar talent that saves us (or whatever

keeps the curtain rod in the wall).

How are you?

I'm good. My armpits are caving in, though.

Laughter splits us.

We agree: eating chocolate ice cream is cannibalistic;

my teacher has shoes older than me;

and Mr. Bergamen lets anger devil his face.

I pray to god he won't be my fourth grade teacher.

What would granny say, us using her panties for parachutes?

Let's land somewhere where

we are lost and found,

new water and argyle mitten,

a map from day-to-day.

From many shells we crawl,

no porcelain tub fills with crashes.

We whistle from every jar,

scrap a moment with shine and ditties.

I smell you; we are that close—

how granny say—

like those good times when I was your age.

Portrait painter

He's a boy raised
by everyone else's
mother. I'm to hold still
on the plastic-covered sofa,
cheekbones steady
for the charcoal's capture.

I'm a girl relocated
from granny's house
to help with younger siblings.
No more time for
double-dutch games
burning my calves.

Today the subject
of an artist's interest—
my hands he discovers
pause to study.

Bastards do this
when their relationship
is not burdened by chores—
look for the way blood
shapes us similarly.

Will he see
where my body forks
and speaks a coolie father
I don't know?

It's different
how our mother looks at us
with sweet and brick
of romances gone.

For Jamar
she turns 14 again,
practices standing
on firm ground
at the moment his father
found a yes
in a no.

She stares at me,
asking, *Why
didn't you kick the habit?*
Shows me the tree
strengthened with years
of abandonment.
My eyes look
like him the most.

I believe I'm not pretty.
Haven't held myself
still to know.
My brother sees
my discomfort—clear
and clean the window
into me drawn.

What do I look like?
He tells me,
*Trust me,
you'll know.*

CHORE

Arriving past midnight, our mother sees her messes:
in the sink, on floors and counters, in the bed;
wakes and tells us, *I'm getting rid of you all.*

No humor beneath her face;
her posture doesn't soften.
Half-staff, she pledges
her hands are done; we're a waste.

Next day, we pack before leaving
to eat breakfast in the school's cafeteria.
Take only what you need, she says. We place
duffle bags on well-made beds. Maybe
she will see yesterday was a slip.

Who hears a teacher after this?
Or the she-said, he-said; and *Yes,
I'll trade my chocolate milk for your white.*
Hanging out on the tire swing after school
is a big no. Ibert's hand in mine,
we cross on WALK, take steps
like each one a petal—will she, will she not?

We're fresh out of flowers, and I believe her.
My brothers beg, *We'll do better, promise.*
The elevator descends to the parking lot
and rings tighten around my chest.

We're a procession of sorry and sadness
led to her car. We know about foster care
from the news, and it's difficult
keeping siblings together.

Why she breaks us, I can't understand.
Bursts into laughter and then tells us,
Next time I'll be serious.

ON THAT DAY

the uniformed men told us we were coming with them.
I was too busy getting Kayana ready, I didn't notice
I was still in my pajamas, and the hairstyle you did
the other day needed to be combed.

You woke up from the anesthesia, took the train half drugged.
On that day, Jamar, me, and Ibert sat in the air-conditioned police station
drinking apple juice. The white cops told us, *Better not see you here again.*
They laughed. We imagined Kayana alone in the hospital shaking.

On the train you fell asleep, opened your eyes
just before our stop. We wondered where you were
while rubbing goose bumps down, watching pistachio
paint peel, listening to our hunger come.

On that day the apartment was too quiet a place
for living children, you cried, and we let our minds wander.

Your head begged for bed; you called
your best friend on that day and asked her to get us.
Walked on legs withering beneath you
to Kayana in the hospital five blocks away.

Later in Angie's doorway, Ibert hugged your thighs,
rested his head between your legs. We shouted,
Where you been? On that day, without a reply,
we calmed our excitement to enter your hush.

P.S. 21'S ASSEMBLY FOR THE BLACKFACE DOCUMENTARY

"I felt that somehow I had to live in the world that the mask created." Kara Walker

I.
At first I refused to be dared.
Jamar's mouth jesters:
I bet you can't throw-up if you stick your finger down your throat.

What's funny makes my classmates tear,
my brother's spittle pearls in my eye,
their drool spots their uniform.

His laughter, a red kerchief,
paints a bull's-eye on my chest.
They charge by the dozens: eyes, tongue, and hands lost.

How then do we make sense of these men
and women blackfaced back in slave days with no
context for why is this the movie for Friday's assembly?

Faced with my belly's contents, my brother knew
a flipped birdie to peristalsis would prove him right—
he's older and badder than me.

He stands there with no pride of extended hands,
C minors *stupid, dumb, dumb, dummy.*
My favorite T-shirt spoils beneath my chin.

The principal shouts, *This is not funny!*
from the projection's jig. Her authority can muffle
giggles, but we know jokes can divide
perforated seams under proper weight.

II.
My brother's face is this screen of black men, hoot in fright.
Our stepfather is a drunk gait to their bedroom.
He fumbles the dark, the lamp to shatter.

Commands my mother to rise; her refusal courts his aggression.
I, foot in front of foot, go expecting my brother to follow.
For all his talk, he lies like all of Bing's hands.

From the hold of my shell, I rip: *Leave her alone!*
Iridescent in the sleep of their eyes,
their pause tests yellow or stone—
My mother laughs....

The sum of me spills like jacks,
like green beans from granny's hands,
like a penis from briefs to shrivel in the thick *haha* of her throat.

Is it me or the business of saving her a knee-slapper?

When mammy's put to care for the master's children,
the boy sitting next to me, with patches on his pants,
catches his breath behind ashy knuckles. He wilts

like the girl in the door frame who's withdrawing
her deposits for rainy days when mammy
brushes past her to get a dustpan and broom.

III.
His grin rises and shines against the door frame,
left-footed in the cat's cradle of his humor.
Every move I make my stepfather watches
me tie my shoe, smooth down my uniform.

Parodies me coming into their room last night:
Leave her alone nigra linguas between his cheeks,
he strokes like a well-groomed goatee. My voice
mimicked to a chick's play at lion.

My mother and brother's laughter webbed with marionette strings,
enough kowtow to let him know their knees can Crow.
For that my brother gets 10 dollars, my mother kissed on the cheek.

I trail backbone and arms on my walk to school;
instinct to care shelved, in the back, away from anyone's violins.
Blend my scales until laughter is panoply against touch,

enter the doors of P.S. Crispus Attucks
and assemble with other 4th through 6th graders,
learning to be fatuous little niggers.

IT'S NOT THAT MY BROTHER WAS ACTING LIKE A FOOL,

it's that he was completely committed to the joke,
gesturing and jumping like a man on the sun—I could
hear the singe of his feet, see the sweat dripping,
his face in shock—that while suspended for seconds,
before his foot touched the sun again, my body
laughed and my laughter laughed and I felt
where suffering had no place.

IBERT'S SICK

My mother splits the cotton ball mitotically,
inserts it in the ear that dribbles hydro-peroxide.
My brother flinches, her fingertips linger like leeches.

The scar: swollen strait of keloid flesh,
runs from earlobe over jugular's pulse.
Doctors serrated him open
to test why the two siamesed knots
swell to the size of his fists.

My mother and I go to the Children's Hospital;
happy to see us come with pizza, we stay
until his sleep is marked by drool on the pillow.

She, to his shoulders, brings the covers.
Stitches woven in like barbed wire make his flesh pucker.
I kiss him goodbye. We leave him in the dark.

Now my mother wraps this diagnosed rare condition;
the same flannel shirt he wore a few months ago
yokes the Tiger Balm heat to his neck.

He leans, adjusting to the elephantine limb
that holds head to shoulders.
He talks and one eye meets mine.

I step close, lassoed by camphor and fever,
to hear words mouthed into collarbone:
Bring me back 10 Sour Powers, Risa.

He's eight and I walk to school alone
with another candy request
for the second time this week.

HELICOPTER, HELICOPTER PLEASE COME DOWN.
IF YOU DON'T COME DOWN, I'LL SHOOT YOU DOWN.

It's hard beneath a heavy hand,
beneath the touch of god
with a mother who cautions,
Your sensitivity is like a broken leg.

Ripped into pieces, those pieces ripped
halfway down the middle,
a sheet of paper makes eight
helicopters whirl six stories down.

The sigh in my chest
matches the falling.

The kids open their hands,
grown folk catch storm
for what they think is trash,
then stop, consider like eyes
before a body disrobes—
what's this, what's this underneath:

A sky loosing its weaving,
returning lashes without wishes granted,
singing the water needed to grow a child...?

They watch like I have shaken
their world and all of sudden
snow in June and still it's hot.

I have chosen Corinthians to shred,
chewed the purple leafs
my mother keeps between the pages
to remember her place.

Weather is breezy; helicopters, dervish;
and everyone, the opposite of sirens.

Take aim

A boy bullets the sky; he doesn't notice the crowd
tracking items to identify him. I name myself with him.

In the trigger, our fingers strike against the days
born with little separation.

We are colder beneath this surviving sun
of a god and goddess who birthed 10.

We need the steadiness of the archer's hand
before he stopped and registered the cost of each fall.

We are wary children; I'm no stranger than this boy
wearing a wife beater—I know the wife beater.

What tundra could be worse?

At eleven years old the taste of each morning
is ice, the heart's antartic on the tongue.

From this season's primer, I've learned
to shovel into a pile and wait for the blow.

The brumal forest in me curtsies
when my stepfather's face takes the bullet.

This is the day when women sit with legs uncrossed—
no men, no need for ladylike—polishing arrows.

YOU SMELLIN YA'SELF, GAL?

Jackie comes knocking on the door on Saturday morning; we don't let her in. She stayed out partying all night and apparently has lost her keys. Velvet black dress with a gold sash, her high-heel shoes in hand. I know she smells like Heineken, a backyard, and five spliffs in one. She's sucking on her teeth, loud and sharp; I step back and lift Ibert to the peephole.

Jamar says, *Be quiet. Let's pretend we're not home.*

We pretend, hold giggles behind our hands, but she knows we're here. We can't go to the pool if she doesn't come. Niesey—our mother's nickname—came in after work on Friday, stayed for about two hours, and during her time with us, said, *Make sure Jackie goes with you to the pool.* Jackie, standing in the kitchen, sucking on cold sugarcane, said, *Me fi got no bathing suit.* We let Niesey know that we could go alone; we've done it before. Jamar's 15, and we'll all pay close attention to Kayana.

Niesey remained expressionless, turned to her sister-in-law and said, *You can wear a T-shirt and shorts, it'll be no problem. People do it all the time.*

Jackie shrugged and said, *OK.*

But why would we want to take this woman to the local pool and she doesn't even have a proper bathing suit? She gets wet, everybody will see her titties in the white T-shirt she wants to wear. We'd barely have a good time minding after Kayana so she doesn't drown. Or starts interacting with people and then people will want to know what's wrong with her. Or she'll throw a tantrum about wanting ice cream but we won't have money for that, and then I'd wind up spending that dollar I saved for situations like this so she'll stop being embarrassing . . . and now add Jackie.

She's Bing's twenty-something sister; came here two months ago from Guyana. Bing's been in prison since February for something that Niesey won't tell us about, and ever since he's been gone, she doesn't come home some nights. When that happens, it feels like I started the day and the sun never came up.

Since Niesey's not here, Jamar's in charge. We're the quietest we can imagine ourselves. I feel each muscle ball up; each pulse sways me. Eventually we go back into the bedroom, close the door, and turn the volume low on the Saturday morning cartoons. Kayana is quiet too. We've threatened not to give her chicken nuggets if she makes a sound. It works. Jackie hammers the door, kicking and cursing. And when she's quiet, I believe she shapes herself into a key or stares into the peephole to fish us out. We're good at making ourselves invisible; you can sometimes see us in strong sunlight, floating about.

Noon comes and we get to cleaning. Jackie hasn't banged on the door for a few hours now. Still, as a precaution, we clean without making noise. But there is something in us that needs to break the silence; it needs more volume, so the broom drops, a pot falls, one of us shouts for one of us and then remembers. A lot of *Ja, I, Ri* happens; we could make a beat if our calls weren't so far apart. Plus, we keep checking on Kayana, making sure she is entertained, giving her dry Froot Loops, reminding her to *shhh,* and so we get to say *shhh* whenever that thing in us needs more sound.

It's Ibert's job to take out the trash. We all listen to the door to hear if it's living or dead. Jamar checks the peephole and doesn't see her. Nothing, and so it's safe. But to make sure he is good, we keep the door open and stand by it. Jamar tells me to go with him but I say no. I tell him he is older and he says something about *being in charge* and *needing to stay with Kayana.* Whatever. He's just as punk as me. But Ibert *has* to go. He speeds down the hall, even in tight Lee jeans and house slippers. We both relax when we hear the incinerator door close.

The elevator opens. We pause and look at each other, my breath is going in and out, in and out, cool and meaty like a Fruit Ice. I see a glimmer of the gold sash, and I know she senses the door is open. Her steps turn to running. Jamar shouts to Ibert, he grabs me by the shirt, slams the door closed, locks the two locks, and puts the chain on. We are lit like lampshades from the rush.

Ibert is still out there.

He screams, *Let me in.*

Jamar opens the door with the chain still on. I look through his legs, his ankles smell like warm scalp and the baby powder that keeps his feet from stinking. Jackie holds Ibert in a soft headlock. He elbows her in the stomach and in her privates. Jackie's not fazed. She's pissed and says something like:

. . . I vex . . . Test me, nuh?
. . . fuckin bomboclots . . . .That's never good.
Maybe . . . ragamuffin, rathole chil'ren.
Gwon knock dis fuckin door down!

Jamar says something like:
You should've came home at a decent hour!
Whatever with your Jamaican-talk. Go back to where you came from.
You so black I really can't see you. . . . That's weak.
Give us Ibert first, and we'll let you in.

Jamar is ridiculous, raging through a crack, with a door chain pressed on his nose. Her hand chopping air, Jackie points it close to him; he steps back and yells, *Don't be puttin that in my face. I don't know where's that been.*

She looks tired like she's been up all night already fighting for herself. Something inside her switches off, and she begins walking down the hall to the elevator, Ibert towed along.

I tell Jamar we can't let Ibert go with her, *He's not wearing clothes for outside.*

He takes the chain off the door and shouts to Ibert to fight loose. He does. He runs, and I hear Jamar say, *Leave the slipper there, stupid.*

Jackie gets him again and drags him onto the elevator.

I'm nervous we're going to get in trouble when Niesey comes home and Ibert's not here. Then I think that Jackie is taking her anger out on him, and I feel this heavy night inside me: clouds spread thin and furrow. The streetlights go on. I feel one car circling so slow it whispers. I can see how if I keep this feeling in me for long a lake can grow. Right in the center of my chest. It'll ripple some days; be a mirror on others; be good for ice-skating when cold. Jamar is trying to figure out what to do; I see him making eights in his thinking.

Let's wet our bathing suits and pretend we went to the pool, and if Niesey comes home, we say Ibert and Jackie went out for somethin.

Somethin what?

I don't know, he says. *Do we need anything in the house?*

We always need somethin in this house, I respond. *But what if Niesey comes and they come and they're not gonna have somethin?*

We stare at each other like a difficult math problem and we both want to get a gold star.

That's dumb—and you're in high school. That won't work. Ibert is only eight, and Jackie don't know nothing, and we have to rescue him.

I know. He folds his arms like a soldier.

I go to the windows in the living room, being sure not to drop a hair or leave a print on the good furniture we're not supposed to be near when Niesey's not home. I look out into the courtyard, and there are three kids playing on the jungle gym. I open the window, take a deep breath so deep I sniff the trees, the brownstones lean in my direction, the kids lift off the ground. I exhale a giant, *IBERT!*

Jamar grabs my arm, he looks me serious in the eyes, *Stop that screamin, dang. Jackie has to come back here. It's a matter of not gettin in trouble for all this.*

The kids in the courtyard look up to our fourth floor window, and I step away so they can't see me, and Kayana peeks into the living room to see what's going on. All this seeing makes me want to hide in a wooden barrel.

Can you just wet the bathing suits and stop buggin out? Jamar begs.

I can't decide between the bathing suit with balloons or the solid blue. I have to match the right one with my mood to make the moment truer. And since I was originally happy about going to the pool, I decide on the balloons. For Kayana it doesn't matter so much and Jamar and Ibert each have one pair of trunks—it is easy.

I put the bathing suits in the bathroom sink and let the water run until they bubble up, then I push them back down. Check the water level and then decide to cut the faucet. Each bathing suit gets wet like we spent all afternoon in pool water, like there were springs in our words and we had a real good time. The day went easy and maybe perfect, like we loved each other. Soaking up so much imaginary chlorine and fun, the fabric goes limp. I wring them out and they don't sing. I toss them over the shower curtain rod. They look sad without our bodies.

I close the bathroom door and the doorbell to the apartment goes ding-ding. Banging that sounds like handballs come with half a breath between. Ibert is at the door. Jamar runs out of the bedroom, reaches the door first, unlock, unlock, unchain and I pull Ibert in. Jamar closes up the door. Ibert has been running for sure. His house slippers have street on them. He's hunched over, hands on his knees. His bottom lip moist from licking, the sweat in beads. He looks up at us; we look down, waiting for him to say what happened.

She took me to Fulton Park. . . . He breathes in and shows his fangs and licks his upper lip. My brother looks a little like a gremlin before it gets wet. . . . *she said she had to pee so she took me to Fulton Park.*

What? You're lyin. We both say.

For real ya'll, I'm not lyin. He stands up now, meets us straight. *She holdin my hand and in the other hand she has this huge pipe. She told me she would run after me and beat me with it if I tried to run away.*

I laugh so hard my sides tighten. Jamar looks at him like he's a trout, nodding his head no.

I ask, *Where she get the pipe from?*

In the back of the buildin. There was a big pile of stuff they took out of an abandoned buildin or somethin. And she saw it there. He puts his hand over his eyes to keep himself from seeing the memory. *It was so embarrassin—she was pickin through the trash and people lookin at us, and I'm tryin to play it like I'm not with her but she's holdin my hand so tight you can't believe.*

Jamar flashes a toothy grin, looking a little like a black version of the kid on the MAD comic books, except Jamar might have more space between his teeth. *You were gone for almost an hour.*

We walked down Marcus Garvey for a long time, and she was talkin about how people was treatin her so bad here. Then mumblin to herself stuff, and I didn't really get all she was sayin. Ibert pauses for a moment and clears his face of any emotion. *I think people at that party she went to last night was mean to her.*

The three of us stand with that for a moment. We know about people being mean. I'm wondering what happened to her last night. And was she rude to those people and they just gave her a taste of her own medicine?

Ibert doesn't allow our heartstrings to be pulled too long and adds, *She's crazy, I'm tellin you because one moment she is kind of OK then she's angry and then starts pullin on me by my collar.*

And now that he mentions it, I can see the neck of his shirt is bent out of shape and looks dirty.

She screamin and cryin, Oh Lord why did you send me here—I was thinking that too. He wipes his face with his too small T-shirt that shows off his belly button.

What happened with you and Jackie goin to Fulton Park? Jamar wonders outloud.

Ibert has a habit of getting off track with his stories sometimes; he gets so excited with talking that he follows the words like crumbs without care for where they're taking him.

I pass by him to go into the kitchen to get some juice, because all of this is making my throat dry. Ibert looks over his shoulder and asks me to get him a cup too and I do.

Yeah, we go in the park. I hand him a cup of Minute Maid Fruit Punch. He sips before speaking. *She takes me over to a bush. And you know Fulton Park isn't that private or anything, so it's not like the bush is keepin people from seein us.* Jamar and I agree, nodding our heads. *She puts the pipe down, pulls down her panties and starts peein right there. And she's still holdin my hand and won't let go.*

She peed right there in broad daylight like that? Jamar covers his mouth.

That's so nasty, I say and take the last gulp of fruit punch.

But I kept pullin and twistin my hand out of her hand. He starts to do what he did with Jackie, how he unscrewed his hand out of her hand. *And I got loose and jetted down the block.*

Oh man, I'm glad you didn't get hit by a car. I'm wary about cars since getting hit by one three summers ago. So it's nice he survived the traffic.

Me too.

After letting the details simmer for a bit, Jamar says, *I can't believe she peed in broad daylight like that with a pipe on one side, and you on the other. That's crazy.*

I know. Ibert turns around to go put his cup in the sink. *Maybe that's what they do in Guyana.*

Don't leave your dirty cup in my clean sink. You better wash it, Jamar says to Ibert. Ibert obeys.

And just as I'm about to ask what do we do if Jackie comes back, the doorbell rings. I quickly look through the peephole and see that Jackie is standing there with the security guard from downstairs. I turn around and let Jamar and Ibert know.

Shit, Jamar says low and breathy because he's not supposed to be cursing, but I think it's appropriate for the moment and Ibert sort of looks at me, wide eyed, holds his smile in, his dimples betraying him.

Open up, I know you kids inside there. I saw the little one running pass just a few moments ago. The security guard's voice is serious and in charge and he looks like the police and so we must behave and be proper and obedient. We stand up straight, fix our clothes, and I straighten my hair a bit. We are about to get in trouble, so we need to primp our innocence.

Jamar opens the door and the security guard is standing on the left and Jackie's on the right, and her face is sunken. She's been crying.

What's wrong with you kids? The security guard waits for us to answer, but I don't have an answer. And what kind of question is that anyway to be asking us. *Why're you locking her out the apartment and you know she's new to this country and has no place to go? This is her home while she's here.*

We stand there totally ashamed, and I can't look either of them in the eye. Jackie isn't

34

looking at us either. I want this moment to go by quickly so I can begin to erase it. We choose silence as our response. Ibert can't hold his giggles in; he's trying really hard to be respectful but it's too much for him to bear and he laughs out loud. Covers his mouth like no one noticed the jack that came out of his box.

You think this is funny, son?

His no is soft and round like a cotton ball.

Last night someone stole her purse and roughed her up a little and all she wanted to do was get home.

As he says this, his voice echoes through me. And to get away from the guilt, my heart drops to my feet.

I think it's best that you let her in and stop playing games. He steps aside and gestures for Jackie to walk into the apartment. We step aside like synchronized swimmers and let her in. *I think you all owe her an apology. She was sitting outside of the building crying. It's no reason for you all to be treating her like that.*

And together we say sorry as Jackie walks pass and directly into the living room. The plastic covering on the couch sighs beneath her body. I think we meant our sorry. I meant it because I hate when people cry or get hurt. If I could drain the well that holds a person tears, I would.

Now, I hope you all can have a good rest of the afternoon. He walks away. Jamar locks the door. I hear the security guard's footsteps become smaller and smaller until I wouldn't notice the difference between his sound and a pin's. Jamar and Ibert have gone into the bedroom and stationed themselves in front of the TV.

Jackie hasn't moved since sitting; she has made herself into a hill on the couch, staring through the windows, but she's looking at the buildings and houseplants inside of her. I don't go near her; I remain in the foyer where we've been for most of the time. The apartment door to my back; the kitchen to the left; the long hallway that leads to our bedrooms and bathroom to the right; the living room in front of my heart. My hands are ready to carry tears. She is sniffling and when she turns around to see me standing there, the red in her eyes is alarming. I stop, feeling caught by her. I look at her for real and notice how she and Bing have the same high cheekbones, a dark brown that is almost edible, flawless, a color that with water and seed can make a flower. Lashes like many, many magician's wands, tiny but still full of abracadabra. She doesn't seem so fiery any more, and something about seeing her soft doesn't make her bad. Maybe pretty even, now that she's not coming after me to pull my ear or strike me for not washing the dishes right. I can breathe and I do.

 She gets up. And for a moment, I think she's coming to hit me because she stops in front of me and watches me like I'm a sea creature at the aquarium. I hear Jamar and Ibert laughing at something that happened on TV, and she says, *Why* you *fi treat me like a dog, nuh?*

She didn't want an answer. She makes her way to the bathroom. And I couldn't give her one if I tried. *We were playing* didn't feel like the match to her question. *I'm sorry* had holes in it. *Maybe you should be nicer to us, because that's what you get* turned the tables and it was never good when someone got hurt. *We are tired of people bossin and beatin us around and then not letting us have fun on our own terms* was so vulnerable that I avoid that road. But I want to say something to her, whatever 11-year-old me could say to grown-woman her. I have all the buds of speech ready to bloom. I am a little angry, a little sorry, and I want to be cool about the whole thing, but I want her to hear me.

I walk the stretch of hallway, pass our bedroom where Jamar, Kayana, and Ibert are lying on their stomachs, on the floor, in front of the 13-inch TV, their faces glowing. They see me pass and Jamar asks, *Risa, what you doing?*

Nothing.

I walk towards the bathroom and the shower is going. Jackie left the door cracked open. And I sit down by it, waiting for her to be done. The water from our bathing suits has made four small puddles that slowly join together; Jackie's dress drinks a little from each, the most from mine. Her leg catches my attention like someone snapped their fingers to wake me from daydreaming. She's scrubbing her foot, then the next, and her humming blends with the shower. She turns around; her butt is two loaves of bread, and I smile at that thought of a baker taking these black bread loaves out of the oven in the early morning when the sun is barely there but so much drama of color is setting us up for its arrival, and the dough is hot and the smell is sweet in the way that babies sometimes smell. She doesn't have big titties like Niesey, hers are sugar cones with the tips dipped in fudge. She looks free, unlike some women who act like their bodies are cages and their eyes are looking out from behind bars. Niesey looks that way most of the time, like she's waiting for the right man to pass, who happens to have the key, so she can step into herself. Jackie is beneath an open sky and the world is hers alone and nobody really can take that from her. Even the guy who took her purse and roughed her up a bit. I wonder if she bathed outside when she lived in Guyana, and what was it like without the stare of skyscrapers, the constant busyness of the streets; what did one hundred crickets sound like?

Why are you lookin at her take a shower for? Jamar taps on my head; the door closes slightly.

I stare up at him with nothing to say. I have to adjust as if I stepped out the movie theater into his question.

Why you being nasty lookin at a girl like that?

I don't think I'm being nasty looking at Jackie. And the feeling of being called out like that makes me want to punch him. *Shut up. I was waitin here for her to come out so I could tell her that I was sorry about today.*

He doesn't believe me. *You can wait in the room.*

I don't want to watch what you and Ibert are watchin.

What, you tryin to like her? Get on her good side so she won't get you in trouble?

No.

The shower turns off and we stare at each other. My heart starts to race and I get up.

Jamar runs back into the bedroom; I run behind him and enter the bedroom with the rest of them. They are watching *Willow* on Channel 11 for the umpteenth time; Kayana is asleep on her bed. Ibert is so captivated by the fantasy world of this midget, wanna-be sorcerer that he doesn't care that we come running in.

Move over. Ibert slides to the left and I join him in front of the TV. Jamar lies on his bed.

Jackie knocks on the door and Jamar says, *Yeah.*

She has the towel wrapped around her body; her hair is wet and pushed back. There are some droplets that hang on the tips of her Jheri curls, some on her cheeks, lips; shoulders. The ones that fall on her face, she wipes away.

Me not like the way you treat me this mornin. It was me intention: come here and bathe and rest, cuz me dealt wit too much fuckery already. She sucks her teeth and tosses her hand dismissively. *Me didn't want to go to the pool wit you. I gwon let y'all have ya fun and do ya ting. And it turns into lockin me from here.* She pauses and looks around the room, avoiding our eyes, then drops her gaze to the floor just before her feet. *Ibert, I treat you crazy-crazy. For that, me sorry.*

Ibert looks up at her. *No problem.* He smiles a little and goes back to Willow who is now meeting Cherlindrea, the queen of the fairies and brownies. He is so easy and forgiving, like a duck the water slides off him.

Lets put this behind us. It don't need to be Niesey's business—promise ya don't lock me from here again? Peace?

Can you promise not to be mean to us? I surprise myself by asking. The words had wings and were itching to fly. Jamar nods his head, agreeing. Ibert too. But they do it ever so slightly to show that they're not fully on my side just in case this all backfires.

Jackie's stare is searching. She's trying to find a puzzle piece inside of me. One moment she had a perfect picture laid out in front of her and then realized a corner was missing. She smiles, moves her head in such a way that means OK and says, *You smellin ya'self, gal?*

I'm quiet. Jamar and Ibert look at Jackie and then me as if this is a tennis match.

You me man and tellin me fi what to do?

I sit beside Ibert wondering, did she wink? Or did she try to close her eye before the water fell in? Whatever she did, I felt a small click.

Maybe you *should take a shower.*

She leaves us to our company, and I can't hold back the smile that wants to show.

AS NEAR AS WE COME TO ANOTHER WORLD

"There're horse bones in the water,"

she says cool and simple,

watches white Friesians leap overboard

in this PBS enactment of the Spanish Armada,

folds her legs and pulls on her polka-dot socks.

She's in shorts and this is the first time

her woman charms me, even if she becomes

that stone, picked from sand, washed

over and over, she calms me.

My skin to her skin is not enough—

orchestrated bumping into and draping onto,

spooning during sleepovers,

huddling when scary movies are on—

I need closer, an infrastructure to get there faster.

I'm her best friend from next door.

I envy the boys who get to take her

on the roof and kiss; she lets them

put hands up her shirt. She smiles,

grown and fresh; her eyes sink

into him pressed on her,

he wanting all the bases.

Everyone says she is bad and up to no good—

her mother, mine, her family, mine, the pastor;

the chatter is the shame in themselves,

lets them turn eyes blind to the brother

who sneaks into her bed.

I do my homework at home;

I'm too much into her plus me,

the ballet she learns at the community center,

her pink leotard, her scent stronger than before.

She is beautiful as all things are

when time is taken to come by

after school, sing high-pitched with the radio,

to listen by the window when her mother's

beating her again. Every door is slamming.

She's fed-up and cries on the 6th floor landing;

she's running away again. I love her will

and if a wish were between us,

I'd want her

to have the longer end.

AN ALBATROSS TO US BOTH

Coney Island, Brooklyn: 1992. Known as "the storm from hell," a northeaster with hurricane-force winds submerges New York City under 4 ft. of water.

Against this we hold our bodies taut

we wear each other like amulets
against come what, come may

we don't muster a hush

our percussive living disruptive
to each sound the waves carry

when they are soundless we worry.

Ibert finds twenty dollars beneath the boardwalk.
we are locked out. our mother too busy to make keys.
we stuck until evening to roam the hallway and beach.

we curse her for forgetting over French fries and franks.
there is wind and ocean to listen to. this is not calm.
it is her voice replaced when it comes no more in the dark.

You can see their circles
stretched or condensed

its movement leads
back to itself over itself

I tell my brother
when you trace too hard
you leave grooves in the looseleaf

we do not sleep tonight

mother and him are making circles
she more so than he
will bear the imprint of his rings

we tell each other the best rides are the ones that go 'round.

We are turning the Ferris wheel with our marathon.

the amusement parked down the street is closed.

the winter leaves the freaks unemployed.

prostitutes stand between the arcade and Nathan's.

the awnings keep them from rain.

Run, she says. run we do.

this gray day shades her bruises.

If you run with me, I promise this will change.

we ferry over the Hudson.

she runs with this.

we run for a dawn-dusted lie.

Swelling the streets since morning, the Atlantic bullies the curbs.

Where are you?

The bus cannot drive through these rivers; I tread the avenues
to the apartment we left days ago.

In its rooms, I return to find not you. From the door ajar,

I call between wind and water, adrift. If this
remained home, we would be eating ramen in school uniforms.

This storm's an albatross to us both.

Coney Island drowns
                    open-mouthed clowns
                                        not quick to bust their balloons.

Heavy with the silk of this sea,
out of this Hurrah's nest, my legs oar. The temper
of these clouds cannot knife our anti-Gallican hitch.

The subway predicts me something:

you,

a neon buoy in the ill-lit Stillwell,
waiting for the water to bring me in.

SHELTER ON STATEN ISLAND

I spend day and night on the balcony, looking at the cranes divide the sky
into the trigonometry equations on the test I missed. Ship comes, ship goes.
At four, they lock into beat; Monday they'll pop again from river to land,
their steady motion like long walks without rest that make my left side
go numb, and then, in the hemisphere without heart, I'm alive.

Loose hairs are soothed in plaits down the roll of my head,
and that's order I can relax into, blow tea and sip. The matters of the heart
have its own storage container shipped abroad—cargo brides and valentines
breathe through a hole as fat as a hamster. If lost in transport, insurance
will cover my claims. I know risks are involved. We have to deal
with stupidity and sunshine; hay fever and we have no say; desire
and mother-gotten; and I don't get her problem. I'm pissed, terribly pissed.

Granny knows how much Lawry's seasoning to put in the potato salad
by graceful shakes, yellow mustard for how it turns it a particular hue,
pepper for its arrangement of spots, relish on the whims of her sweet tooth,
and her liking is my liking and I can indulge in food; I prefer it neat on my plate.
Niesey offers ramen and candy—all that could be gotten at the bodega.
Tomorrow she'll find a market. I need to leave—dinner isn't important.
My body can take slight starvation and my mind is moving horizontally,
and no thought can truly get me out of here.

SUBTEXT TO THE MESSAGE SENT VIA THE FRIEND OF THE REMEDIAL BOY WHO ASKED ME TO MY JUNIOR HIGH SCHOOL PROM

Your stare of trying to read a big word,
pronounce this misplaced gifted & talented me,
pulls me to where the other black kids learn,

to frustrated teachers and used textbooks
that make you into the below-average men
whom my mother shares her bed.

Pregnant at fourteen, swayed by a boy
not gentleman enough to take off her coat.
Six kids later, she sleeps with a Jamaican mechanic
who gets drunk and leaves her a bouquet of bruises.

His dollars feed his Jamaican-born children;
she can't afford to get me a prom dress. Remedial Boy,
you are diesel-scented hands, calmed by exhausted pleas.

You could be her first husband, the Guyanese
with the onomatopoetic name. You and I traffic
drugs up and down the East Coast. Polydactyl dreadlocks
pledge our Rasta allegiance. I learn to roll caya in cornhusk,

calculate ounces for dime bags, unwrap hair for contraband
search during jail visits. When you're gunned down, I
grip the gurney, watch blood bead a rosary across your chest.

Remedial Boy, I hold, like two last breaths,
our daughter and son when officers usher you out.
Commit to memory the narcotics officer who spoke
with gun, *Next time I'll take your children away.*

IF YES

The down and afghan
of their love could've sent
my guards to lunch.

I've never seen them
pull close into pits
of the body to feel heat
called up by the presence
of each other near.

No hand on back
smooths down her shirt
until hankering for skin rips
away cotton and he is fingers
in dirt making sustenance
from storm clouds and patience.

No laughter because her laughter
catches in his teeth
and he to show gratitude
for something good and right,
gives it back the way she gave it.

No kisses to lay an unborn
talk on each other's tongue;
no stepping away mute
until their mouths learned to walk again.

MY LITTLE *CHULETA*

The beans are shinier, blacker in water, their skins now split. In the kitchen to get a drink of something, the sun's coming up and the day is still. I've memorized vocabulary words for the Spanish test today. Nigel helped. I pronounced *chuleta* out loud and he stood at the other end of the hallway, supported by the sky-blue ball. I have never seen him this way; he was as foreign as the words in my workbook—I'm better at reading than speaking, and Mr. Gongora can try to correct my pronunciation, but how *I* said it made a baby stand. *Chuleta, chuleta,* he stepped. *Chuleta,* he walked. *Chuleta,* I opened my arms and he ran his life into mine, and I didn't know first steps could flood my heart. Felt good to scream, excited for something not aloneness and another's death. Niesey came from the kitchen, left the beans soaking, alarmed an emergency was happening close on her watch— *What is it?* I'm not supposed to drink juice from the carton but that's what happens with the early bird—you don't see her catch.

THE SMALL PLACES I GO

I hide from the light
beneath the cover of lids,
and where I go is tinted
with the color in which
we mark our errors.
This sadness makes me
stamp size. To linger
in a corner with all
the hush and whisper
I will never find
this part without
absolute quiet and then
what will I do with it?

I prefer the hem of things: the circumference

> of cotton wrists,
> woolen torsos,
> limp parasols of skirts.
> The husk of ourselves
> hang in quiet,
> gestures no want or need.
> I don't like them very much
> on some days, mostly.
> Among these bodies built
> tall and lumbering, I want to ax
> their legs, yell timber,
> to cut my mother's tail
> she chases in the sport
> of catching herself. I can offer
> a quiet fall to each of them.

I landed first between yellow lines,
cushioned by the push and pull
of traffic. When I say my brother's
name, I call him into the crash
and fracture of organ and bone.

It is his decision to let me cross
the street alone. He runs
for mother. And to this day
his sorry remains lost.

When the enclosure is embracing,

                              I imagine no one's arms. There is no heart
                              to the squeeze. It's better
                              when there's no brother
                              who suffocates
                              me with a pillow; I pull breath
                              out of down the way fish
                              get air from water.
                              Like it is better
                              when the lightning
                              is not my mother's.

She has a skirt that looks like a street:
stripes of white run the middle;
she is the vehicle that drives this article.
Across the hips I'm deer-eyed,
holding the road like the only home we have.
I cannot sue her accidents.
What does it matter
when I say, *We do not like him*?
She is a woman of muffled ears.
It's winter when it comes to my words.

This is how I mend
the pain: I take a spoon,
heated on a gas range,
to my sister's thigh. Not a scream
or yell, a glimmer of a jolt.
She is us. Look how we
withdraw from our skin
like underwear, socks, our best school
clothes, and when they are too hard
to wear, we pass them along,
and no one notices the keloids,

the re-stitching in awe
of starch and creases.

When they find me asleep on the closet floor,

                        my brother and sister
                        say, *We heard you talking.*
                        My mother is smiles.
                        Why do they come find me?
                        I need the meters and yards
                        to imagine a blackness that blends
                        me with roads and nights,
                        slips me from the corridors that remind
                        me of how their faces dull
                        the treasured parts I want to keep in shine.

What you come to meet at ends:
ports and shantytowns,
me folded like a note
waiting to toss
myself to any wave
muscle enough to get me back.
Really, what is the point
of the sun's ritual,
the light and heat of its circling,
if what rivers through me
is a hunger—
the drought and flood of it?

TENDERIZED

"Oh we fear our enemy's mind, the shape in his thought that resembles the cripple in our own, for it's not just his fear, but his love and his paradise." Rebecca Seiferle

I fear it all. The fresh morning distilled to imported backwash,
the humidity sleep leaves on the scalp, his hands mastering me into a ring of breath.

In the pearl flesh of her young woman, my mother
worked minutes into making these lungs that can bagpipe for air, but I don't.

The herd of myself wrangled to a waterhole, stationed on hooves
with god-given stripes to come close to the embarrassing curtsey of words.
I offer myself like one of the carved tchotchkes on the mantel.

For the ways I imagined myself vicious,
they're as inanimate as carnival prizes. I barter
my sentinels, concede myself as my mother does to his aggression

—we share more than this face, given to the same expression
when speech is strangled.

I see the subterfuge of her carapace—not only now, even then in that Polaroid:
the seventies, dressed in navy/red rugby, dungarees;
complacent, her grin.

I wanted once to step into that picture; she I thought beautiful
with the hunger of a beloved child.

And like her childhood friends who see her in me,
he hurts me in ways familiar to my mother.

Initiates her facsimiles into this tradition of their years—
meticulous cuts to leech like adolescent clits on my heart.

THE SPELL IS BROKEN

My mother is want of waking;
his kisses the alarm she needs.

Each night, frogs on the doormat.
We've given up city holler for country calm,

Greene Avenue for Shenandoah Lane.
I have thought many times about wings;

the way birds hoist from the ledge,
land with helpings of sky in their beak.

With thoughts of jumping, these frogs come;
ribbit and slime greet toes and arches.

One bold to hop on my foot, watches in wait
for its stomping, for fingers like biology tools

to find the heart, the lungs. I've learned to quiet my hand
when it parts flesh, tame breath in the company

of dead things—we walk around our mother's
sleeping self, pour our sounds in her exhalations,

and hope she doesn't feel us like spider webs
and brush our presence into a ponytail,

or a braid, to be rid of our upkeep. And then, on the day
when the frogs come as no surprise, he is there.

We packed our house in the night to get away
from him. His eyes bulge; the Southern heat turns

his skin moist, walks past me up to her bedroom.
Their cricket calls let us know she hasn't thrown him from her hips.

SISTER

I selected your name from the tagged partition
in the Black Pearl taxicab. Shaquana, the one who defies
in permanent marker, you are bold letters among faded
ink-whispers of people afraid to make their mark strong.

Born to us with six-pointed hands, newborn half fingers
planted with a seed of bone, a possibility of intricate cross hatches
and indelible strokes, an isotopic rising and dipping of terrain.
You lined with a person's symmetry and pointed it right into their face.

On that night, your hands broke the hold Cornel had on me.

>   In my left eye, our mother is statue.
>   Her hands lack dexterity for saving.

>   He's in my right eye, drunk and primed—
>   the man you've disowned as your father.

>   He chokes me into a silence that turns
>   everything purée, telling me he loves me.

>   My eyes focus on you, and you see I am in need.

Your scream cuts the silence;
you lift your arms and the vase cries down.
He releases me to catch blood and glass.

You flee for the police. Shaquana, your flight, my first breath.

JUMPED

Your eyes are as quiet as my feet.
We both are whispers to each other.
You are the most focused I've ever seen you.

> (No, you are this way during mornings
> while we wait for the school bus,
> holding yourself like the flame to the stick's end.
> You are here, here, here until the yellow doors shut.)

I want to think you are blessed with forgetting.

You know, he didn't smile.
She brought him home with little introduction;
we sat in our room painted evening sky, watching TV.

Remember, he mouthed a "hello,"
didn't bring a suitcase, but the linoleum held up his,
closets opened to his, air clung to his;
he locked the door with his set of keys.

I was afraid to take you to the beach.
We lived near Coney Island. Near the ocean,
I thought, *Run in.* That is where we lived,
in the duplex apartment with the mermaid in our address.

We threw laundry bags down the steps.
I see the clean whiteness of them in the dim hallway, as headlights,
your eyes wide. Saliva glints like fishing hook in your cheek.

Heard keys in the door, you a pig before slaughter.
He drags you down the steps.
The more you shout, the more he hits.
Sahree, you manage over again until you are beaten.

I watch your sleep whimper, your face welt.

Remember, together into the arms of those little boys.
You climb into the bedroom window and the guard falls out.
On the ledge, you test the air with your toe.

You think they invite you to play, to pour into the sky.
On three, your hand in mine,
those boys like weeds, on our thighs the sun's warm;
the concrete, salted like boardwalk.

DISPOSITION FOR SHININESS

1.

She can make herself into her own craving.
Each one of us born with her face—
more masculine or feminine.

Each one of us learning how to strike
at the anger inside, given before we
cultivated our own.

Tease the third born about his big head
until he cries and finds security
at the back of her knees.

The fourth, underweight and retarded,
we found ways to distance like nurses
who change the diapers of the elderly.

It's what we do to keep cool: the older one
flicks a melting lighter on my face, laughs
like a jackhammer, and I'm the one
who has her face the most.

She keeps running away from her reflections
like we're telling her to get the switch
for the spanking she is to receive.

Like over and over again, we a post-it
for some stone she had to swallow,
some pain that can't be exfoliated down.

Like the daddy-sized slippers taken over
by gentleman callers or that cocklebur of a mantra:
I will not be like her, I will not be....

Her mother who opted for single parenting
than a gambling husband. We carry this for what?
Like coffin or cradle for that bruised girlchild in her.

2.

I would never raise not a snowflake to her—
give nothing volume contrary to her stomp.
For every scream, its echo remained in
some strange purgatory in my throat,
housed in bottles leafed from trees, there
was no ripeness to let them from the limb,
an orchard of all my mother never heard.

She, behind a globe, took our shouts for goldfish.
There were no quakes on this coast to give
her dense bits buoyancy, she remained anchored
with all her matters at her feet.

She pulls back her hair and there's a widow.
Slicked, she stands at the peak of her thoughts.
Our mother polishes her requiem until it's an opal.
Watch it long, it glistens like a leech. It's a flank of the heart—
coveted like candies at the bottom of her pocketbook.
She has it all together. She has washed down her privacies to a sparkle,
tested them across glass, exchanged sleep for stain-free underpants.

It's frightening how she has an epitaph's unmistaken permanency;
the way the script attempts to smile in marble,
give light to graveness without budge
from repeating this existence joined by hyphen.

On the days we call granny and hang up the phone
when her voice meets our ears to know if it is true—our
mother was borne and not a haunt—we know her answer
is no visor for the smog that rise bright and aubergine
in our mother's skin.

3.

Why does she take this turn in the fork?
Come back with the same set of shiny beans,
a story of how she got them, and what the old woman
said—she can have a perfect man: sun, water, and proper faith.
She introduces him, first name only.
His accent puts him from an island.

Who are we to rid her of glass slippers,
Huxtability, and thereafter?

The young ones are more kind;
the older ones approach him with thorns,
avoid the same rooms. We hate to account for his presence
when friends ask, *Who's that?*

Our mother's boyfriend—
we could have pointed to the man in the park,
in the Knicks jersey, and extended the same courtesy.
The man with the cool Ewings doesn't have keys.

He rarely greets us—
what's the point of saying hello over again?
He stays more nights. This is the beast
crawling down the stalk:

Our doors are not locked to it,
morning or night it has welcome.
No choice to pretend we are not home;
it no longer needs the permission of a fisheye.

She gives it the wheel; not one of us can take shotgun.
Why do we notice the gold in its grin?
In the rearview mirror, we see her lean
back in the passenger seat, her hand on its thigh.
Why do we feel the slack in her defenses?
Hammock fills with too many siesta naps.

She won't hear the inch-by-inch lifting
of glue from the hand—what our spirits do
to tread the shit that mothers this ground.

4.

We are a week together. Sun up, sun down.
We fold the smaller one into the bigger one
until we are one child our mother cannot hold.

What happens when Monday goes away in a plastic bag?
Our brother takes as many as he needs to fit his clothes.
These sacs logoed with a key, inflate like jellyfish.

He can't take it anymore.
How do we fold to fit where groceries go?
Out the door, we follow his footsteps through closets,
into the corner where the cat litters, behind the bathroom sink
the elevator opens. His body leaves a draft.

We speak into the hole of our heart,
and there's nothing to hold the box.
We know this exquisite corpse between us.

We do not make up for the absence of his voice,
survive off missing letters until they're a broken pigeon
clipped and stowawayed in the pockets of those
who have other places to call home.

Monday is one of those troubling days,
a passing or an abuse too grief to start the week.

If we feel what his departure left us,
we will not feel outdated in his hand-me-downs.
We will admit, *It's better without him, more for us.*
Still moored to us, we keep his things as he left them.

5.

You are becoming a lady, she beams.
Gestures to accompany her in her boat
to reminisce over the withered homunculi of her years.

Her touch to my neck inappropriate
since we've gone without affection.
I've learned to trust her like a hive.

We alone together is me, one egg in the pigeon's nest
between my rusting ten-speed and brick wall.
The wind blocked my body from her.

Night and day, we were audience
to feathers tossed and shit about.
It's hard to listen to courtship.

She tells me, *With children you will never be lonely.*

For each year the wish for her to love me is broken,
and the cast is old and soiled around my chest.
How does she take notice of breast and not this
need with its own taste and odor in my throat?

I'm becoming woman on thrift. My prepubescence
held in the arms of virginal robes, waiting, waiting
for my mother's will to love me strong.

She tells me to marry a Jamaican.

The nest is never left alone. When the father is absent,
the mother tends the kind of seed who grows tall,
bitter—and I'm exacting when kicking the egg.

6.

Behind what thicket sipping what dram of what
in the amphitheater of whose canyons
did you find yourself neighbor to your heart?

Equipped your mouth with empty mountains to meet
one random frequency shucked from frost and barbed wire,
from behind and in suites of folded arms—you finally heard?

Now not interned in the tango of yourself,
you call to this flag you loomed threadbare
but the watermarked gauze is not fit to hold tears.

I struggled with *and* when learning to read—

this conjunction between hailing memory and weathered organs,
and what is to follow those impossible ellipses:
May beetles or some excruciatingly beautiful zion?

And what—an inquiry that shows no other side.
This is all applause I offer the pink horse
come to bed fetal in my discs, dulling my epaulets.

I'm tired of my figments running my filaments down.
Your apology deserves no purple hearts or soldiers
in tight formations with solemn mouths.

Rush me back to bed this lethargy has taken my legs!
I remix your rueful ballads until I break
necks on your conditional retrospectives.

Ask why until your tongue can't pick up sticks,
until the glue and rubber step aside
say, *It hurts like the cradle and all, mother.*

Let's meet on the right morning when our beast
find us not suitable prey; your crew, my crew,
one wish from our urchin of lashes,

And our customs to the dust we pirouette down.

RIBBONS AND STRAW

On mornings like this I find her shirts and pants puddled at her feet, my mother sewing. The knit and stitch of parted skin puckers. Stuffs back into herself the ribbons and straw that fattens her. She hums a note, starved for more sound, I hear like a baby

I touch my insides over and over until I'm something I can put in my mouth—it's frightening to think my mother belongs to me. I see her walk down the street, crushed between King James's lips, and when she's close enough to grab my hand, she's a box of buttons

I'm lonely for my life in her hands, my mother—who cannot rescue her heart from the barrel of her chest—always stealth in her love, always without the proper ear, without the proper conduit, without the sand pearling between her toes, without her calendar of holidays, without her Magdalene at her feet

She looks best when mortar, when I trust her to hold things together. In navy she sails. Returns and the notch on the doorframe has gone from here to there. We meet each other with owls in our mouths

The first to show me a pomegranate, how to eat one. Red breast in her palm, she sliced into quarters. Peels off the white skin, gently, like a woman's shirt. Her collar blushes at fourth touch

The sun brings down its shade, she lies asleep; I pull back her skin and lick the butter

She is a season of too much salt. Guarded in her swim, she's a strange monarch washed in waves. Her bramble hair and brand new coils have tailored the fence around her face. Always, always I'm fumbling to unlock the grief. I've given too many cards for the refrigerator door; she's a magnet for one

I tell people I leave only intentional trails. I leave my mother in the crowd; she calls like Grand Canyon's want to fill. Pulls and persuades my body no injury will come of this welcome

Nowhere will nest me. Glass holds a signature of letting go. She stands between a blow; her body smarts, learns it cannot take the same intensity. Her emotional wells. Her towel-cape. She cries over her toes

I hold her like an artery above a river.

RAW MEAT MAKES MY HANDS AWARE OF THE SKIN'S UNRAVEL

        To his heart
        I a deep plunge
        who cannon balls
        the glass
        shell of a lake

: *For try it*,
his sleeping face challenges.

I step with the gentleness of wiping
my baby brother's circumcised penis.

The knife smells of onion,

moles like crows on the bough
of his cheek;

I look for the line, the hook
that tears the roof of my mother's
mouth—

nothing
for what is it she sees?

He rolls and shifts to his side,

my brother's 40-year-old stare,
waking.

STARVED

1.

She won't let me in the kitchen. I scrape evidence of her bad cleaning into my fingernails. Cornbread on the left. Fried chicken on the right. In my pockets, my hands fist. She checks them now, vacuums the corners and countertops. Takes to cutting my nails, but there's nothing when she comes with clippers.

2.

The air thickens
when the sun comes hot
gravy thick
flecked with pepper
beef brown
pangs
rest quiet

The ice cream truck
can't wake it.

3.

On her belly she rubs circles
the way I do at night,

to quiet the begging.
She is growing a child for herself;
it's making her fat.

I pray for my own—
its arms and legs;
the gristle of torso and head,

for my chest to grow
the baby's milk
from my breast—I suck.

4.

Spring and summer make the trees green
but it's fall when they're ripe.

5.

      Down my throat, the ink is sauce;
the pen is chisel for a patch of paint.
From the hall, maple veneer splinters into toothpicks.

A cumulus of cotton candy in the walls
      takes saliva from the next swallow,
      turns hunger to sleep and my ear
      to the innie recounts not one groan.

I chase a pigeon into my hands;
we match in heart. The beat makes the thirst
for yellow forgotten. Feathers; belly first, I break
no fruit similar to its pulp.

6.

Winter's a clean plate.
The plows reveal
a stove's insides blank.

7.

I'm practicing
to breathe my
smell to nothing.
My bones will faint—
this house, my shoes
will empty.

UNDER THE CIRCUMSTANCES
For Kayana, Shaquana, Nigel, Uriah

It holds me strong; the grief is all the rain I need.
I'm sorry for leaving you in the house alone,
my heart had no more shatter, only room to bleed.

It happened similar this way before: Cornel calls,
hangs up. Repeatedly. He slurs, wants Niesey;
she's not here. Last time, he broke in.

The dust is unsettled in this wound.
Niesey enjoying Reb Lobster won't leave—
You're overreacting; Cornel isn't coming to the house.

I pace the apartment; every corner his hands
grab for my throat, and each one of you
peaceful in a dream my body can't imagine.

Friends tell me to get out of there. Say, *She'll rush
home if you're not there.* It's not my absence I wanted
her to come home to, but to me. I needed to know

she would save me; she would show up—this time.
For all my years, I have given her little trouble,
barely back-talked; I'm the least of her worries

when the entrée is served. I keep going to voicemail.
Her ways are not a turn in my direction.
It's clear and obvious: step out of the road.

THE EMPEROR'S SOCKS

Around his ankles, the color of static twists.
No arches for caterpillars, grasshoppers to shelter
when his foot comes down. He tells me—my mother and siblings
gone off to Disney World—*I walked barefoot when I a boy in Jamaica.*
Brown sugar caramelizes to soot, the first step
to preparing oxtails. *We had no money*, he adds.
Tosses salt over his shoulder before serving it to the meat.

We meet in daylight for the first time in years
outside the tunnels of the railroad apartment.
I throw salt from my skin, his socks in my mouth
make thoughts lose frequency. A sparse alphabet
of gray hairs repeats on his jaw. On bodega awnings,
his eyes flit on what shoes pass us by.
I shift my tuning, adjust a "hello,"
his accent stutters in sunlight.

Curious and barefoot, he's a boy
in his mother's den where the foot is schooled:
smashes daylights like *peenie wallies*,
stomps on backyard, later skulls.
He says the sorry nesting in his eyes.

I know the hook in the eye
we wear to be proper. I was silent—
the last female in the house he beat before I left.
On the first day of college, I unzipped
my luggage and his socks made it with me.
How do I shape this foot to carry
a leaning spine and his apology?

IN THE GRIP OF DIRT

They say an oak has the desire to be an oak

when housed in the grip of dirt

it dares itself to grow—I feel that seed in me.

Some ghosts balance along your curbs,

at the foot of your queen, kneel by

your bathtub—cold hands and loofah

rub touch raw until breath comes out in baby steps,

walks the thrashed and shameful rooms

with mirrors and scales that show you of no wood.

When the therapist asks how I feel,

my statements toddle.

My emotional arithmetic is basic: I'm sad.

That admission brings buzzards close.

My empty hands petition for the angel

left in the snow when I was six, every shoelace snapped

in a rush; the fried chicken that drove my mother

into the next borough when our mouths were one;

the cat that refused to be leashed, but I dragged

her and her will remained unsuffocated.

I tire of coming across thirsty saplings.

Let this nest on whatever station when the knob

turns the heart: listen to the celloist's

serenading symmetry; between her breasts

the curtain parts in your dream tonight.

What is bandage for loss?

Stillness is long haul from sugar cube to anthill,

like each hair, antennae to the oak's will to grow.

YOGA

The wooden flute exhumes the eight-
year-old from my left side, whole and still
stuck before the headlights.

The Toyota sent her
into the other vein of traffic.

Lovers would tell me
from left foot up to shoulder down
I smell of oranges.

Gripping the Sunkist granny peeled,
she bit into twice before it was her body
tossed into the morning, below the lid
of the streetlight, it came down.

In this hemisphere, my grown body
has let her cower, packed tight.
The impact shattered my leg.

The liver, in frantic repair,
seamed itself back together.

The body comes on strong to heal,
and I've kept myself on the curb,
afraid of accidents.

Gone stale, rigid beneath touch,
cautious of a body's velocity—
I have many front lines—
the company of elsewhere soothes my wheels.

Through hoop earrings the road blurred,
my mother turned the dial, this state line
is a different frequency for usual songs.

Give your body permission to rest,
says the instructor, *relax the back of the heart.*

I watched the back of her neck rest
and go taut like double-dutch ropes
in anxious girls' hands.

It's hard enough to wait
for lights to turn red. I'm seeing
my mother again after a week's passing.
Her face is weathered beside the gurney.

Let it go. This directive leaves me unsure—
what will be useful to me later?
My whole life stutters.

I don't move down there on my back,
tires are flutes, slowing down to take breath.

WHAT IS IT WE BURN INTO OUR HEARTS?

The Guyanese woman putting obeah on Kayana. She was someone to blame.
The truth was too much for Niesey to share, she'd say: *Well, when Ibert*

and Kayana was little we went to Guyana and the weather was so hot....
Time goes by and there's no witch revenging her daughter's broken heart.
No record breaking Guyanese summer; countryside shack, or sweet treats

brought to the American and her two American children. It's you
enamored with a sister, asleep in the bassinet beside the bed.
It's summer in Brooklyn; we're living on Fulton Street in the apartment

with concrete floors. Kayana is fresh life, months old; Niesey's in the kitchen
and you are quiet, knowing to hold her soft. Never once did our mother make
you feel what you've forgotten, let you walk across the bridge that links

you to the lesion on Kayana's brain. Two-years old, you didn't know any better.
Many times I wished Kayana normal. If she wasn't that way, there would've been
room for me to dance after school, be in band, hang out longer at the handball

court with friends, chat the streetlights on. Imagine running to beat the setting
sun; the panic of not making it home on time charges the pump in your legs.

I know there's more you wanted to do, but that's the loss of one gesture.
Somehow you're never forgiven for errors, never without the suffering;
delayed like Kayana who cannot count beyond ten, and for your strides,

thinking a different outcome each time, she'll stand there pooling spit.
She is yours; she is ours. This is the pretty from the dominoes' fall.
There are lessons I want to skip; move in the world so I don't unstitch

or freeze another's heart. Come and go scentless—I wasn't alive with my elbows
pulled to my ribs. We've taken on wrong narratives about ourselves to avoid
wearing our hurt. Grief is a numbing heirloom. One pearl at a time, brother,

I'm uncovering and reminding myself this is what I'm doing. I'm bound
to get off track, tell myself, *I'm not worth it—it's all I know*—so I'm uncovering
to the grain, to a mindful way to love.

Arisa White is a Cave Canem fellow, an MFA graduate from the University of Massachusetts, Amherst, and author of the poetry chapbooks *Disposition for Shininess* and *Post Pardon.* She was selected by the *San Francisco Bay Guardian* for the 2010 Hot Pink List. Member of the PlayGround writers' pool at Berkeley Repertory Theatre, her play *Frigidare* was staged for the 15th Annual Best of PlayGround Festival. Recipient of the inaugural Rose O'Neill Literary House summer residency at Washington College in Maryland, Arisa has also received residencies, fellowships, or scholarships from Squaw Valley Community of Writers, Hedgebrook, Atlantic Center for the Arts, Prague Summer Program, Fine Arts Work Center, and Bread Loaf Writers' Conference. Nominated for a Pushcart Prize in 2005, her poetry has been widely published and is featured on the recording *WORD* with the Jessica Jones Quartet. A blog editor for HER KIND, and the editorial assistant at *Dance Studio Life* magazine, Arisa is a native New Yorker, living in Oakland, CA, with her partner.

CPSIA information can be obtained
at www.ICGtesting.com
Printed in the USA
LVOW03s1022020216

473325LV00011B/189/P